LEVEL
3
Fact Reader

Gallop!
100 FUN Facts About Horses

Kitson Jazynka

NATIONAL
GEOGRAPHIC

Washington, D.C.

For kids who love horses as much as I do —K.J.

Designed by Yay! Design

Trade paperback ISBN: 978-1-4263-3238-8
Reinforced library binding ISBN:
978-1-4263-3239-5

The author and publisher gratefully acknowledge the expert content review of this book by Vicki Lowell, chief marketing and content officer of the U.S. Equestrian Federation, and the literacy review of this book by Mariam Jean Dreher, professor of reading education, University of Maryland, College Park.

Photo Credits
Cover, Jeff Vanuga/Minden Pictures; 1, Makarova Viktoria/Shutterstock; 3, Katho Menden/Shutterstock; 4 (UP), Srdjan Stefanovic/Getty Images; 4 (CTR LE), vblinov/Shutterstock; 4 (CTR RT), hidesy/Shutterstock; 4 (LO), Erik Lam/Shutterstock; 5 (UP), Buffy1982/Shutterstock; 5 (CTR LE), Ronald Zak/AP/REX/Shutterstock; 5 (CTR RT), Dan Leffel/Getty Images; 5 (LO LE), gsagi/Getty Images; 5 (LO CTR), eugeneser-geev/Getty Images; 5 (LO RT), Studio 37/Shutterstock; 6, loflo69/Getty Images; 7, Arterra Picture Library/Alamy Stock Photo; 8, seraficus/Getty Images; 9 (UP LE), Zuzule/Shutterstock; 9 (UP RT), GlobalP/Getty Images; 9 (CTR), GlobalP/Getty Images; 9 (LO LE), LOSHAD-ENOK/Getty Images; 9 (LO RT), 66North/Getty Images; 10, Jeffrey Schwartz/EyeEm/Getty Images; 11, CMOgilvie/Getty Images; 12–13, VUSLimited/Getty Images; 13 (UP), Zuzule/Shutterstock; 13 (LO), AP/REX/Shutterstock; 14, kyslynskyyhal/Shutterstock; 15 (UP), MarcCharbonne/Getty Images; 15 (LO), Mark Newman/Getty Images; 16, Polryaz/Shutterstock; 17 (UP LE), bstoltz/Getty Images; 17 (UP RT), Nattika/Shutterstock; 17 (LO), Erik Lam/Shutterstock; 18, Gordon Clayton/Getty Images; 19, olgaIT/Getty Images; 20, zysman/Getty Images; 21 (UP), Jak Wonderly; 21 (CTR), Rowena/Shutterstock; 21 (LO), anakondasp/Shutterstock; 22–23, GlobalP/Getty Images; 24, JohnPitcher/Getty Images; 25 (UP LE), vikarus/Getty Images; 25 (UP RT), olgaru79/Shutter-stock; 25 (LO LE), Abramova_Kseniya/Getty Images; 25 (LO RT), Zuzule/Getty Images; 26–27, starush/Getty Images; 27, Carol Walker/Minden Pictures; 28, PHOTOCREO Michal Bednarek/Shutterstock; 29 (UP), sgoodwin4813/Getty Images; 29 (CTR), Carol Walker/Minden Pictures; 29 (LO LE), Eric Isselée/Shutterstock; 29 (LO RT), Joanne Moyes/Alamy Stock Photo; 30, GlobalP/Getty Images; 31, Marie Charouzova/Shutterstock; 32, Juniors Bildarchiv GmbH/Alamy Stock Photo; 33 (UP), Dziurek/Shutterstock; 33 (CTR), Simon Bruty /Sports Illustrated/Getty Images; 33 (LO), Carrie Antlfinger/AP/REX/Shutterstock; 34–35, Design Pics Inc/National Geographic Creative; 35, Hilary Andrews; 36 (UP), anakondasp/Getty Images; 36 (LO), Pavlo Burdyak/Shutterstock; 36–37, Tim Platt/Getty Images; 38 (LE), Fotokostic/Shutterstock; 38 (RT), Tim Platt/Getty Images; 39, Serge Mouraret/Alamy Stock Photo; 40 (UP), DEFHR; 40 (LO), CHBD/Getty Images; 41 (UP), Steven Cargill/racingfotos.com/REX/Shutterstock; 41 (LO), AF archive/Alamy Stock Photo; 42, REX/Shutterstock; 43, redtea/Getty Images; 44 (UP LE), Nataliia K/Shutterstock; 44 (UP RT), Anaite/Shutter-stock; 44 (CTR LE), Adonna Combs; 44 (CTR RT), Yana Ermakova/Shutterstock; 44 (LO), vovashevchuk/Getty Images; 45 (UP LE), Sportfot/Thierry Billet; 45 (UP RT), GlobalP/Getty Images; 45 (CTR), wildpixel/Getty Images; 45 (LO), GlobalP/Getty Images; Top border (throughout), VectorPot/Shutterstock

Printed in the United States of America
18/WOR/1

Table of Contents

25 Cool Facts About Horses   4

Chapter 1: Horse History   6

Chapter 2: Horse Sense   14

Chapter 3: Saddle Up!   34

25 More Facts About Horses   44

Horse Facts Roundup   46

Index   48

1

Horses can sleep standing up, locking their legs to keep from falling.

2

The oldest known horse, an English horse named Old Billy, lived to be 62 years old.

3

Like most mammals, horses have a belly button.

4

A horse's teeth take up more space in its head than its brain does.

5

Closely related to rhinos and tapirs, horses belong to a group of mammals that have an odd number of toes.

6

Horses belong to the equine (EE-kwine) family, which also includes zebras, donkeys, and mules.

7

A horse's brain weighs about the same as a human child's—about a pound and a half.

8

The term "equine" refers to a horse or describes things having to do with horses. It comes from the ancient Greek word *equus*, which means "quickness."

9

In the late 1800s, European carriage horses wore straw hats to help shade them in the summer.

25
COOL FACTS
ABOUT HORSES

10
Tough Welsh ponies roamed the hills and valleys of Wales, Great Britain, as far back as 1600 B.C.

11
Horses with blue eyes are rare, but they can occur in many breeds.

12
Horses tend to move faster when they are headed home.

13
As many as eight million horses served during World War II.

14
An adult horse produces about 10 gallons of saliva per day.

15

At a world-famous riding school in Vienna, Austria, a stallion is referred to as a "professor" once he's finished his training.

16
Blueskin and Nelson were two of General George Washington's war horses during the American Revolution.

17
Like homeless dogs and cats, many horses around the world are waiting to be adopted.

18
Some horses have wardrobes that include rainproof sheets and fitted blankets to keep them warm and dry.

19
Until the invention of the steam engine in 1698, horses provided the fastest and most reliable transportation on land.

20
A horse's hooves grow about a quarter inch per month.

21
The famous racehorse Exterminator had a series of companion ponies, all named Peanuts.

22
Some birds like to make nests out of discarded horse hair.

23
Horses carried gear across the Rocky Mountains for the American explorers Meriwether Lewis and William Clark.

24
In the timed sport of barrel racing, horse and rider race a cloverleaf pattern around a set of three barrels.

25
Male horses have more teeth than females do, including four extra "fighting teeth."

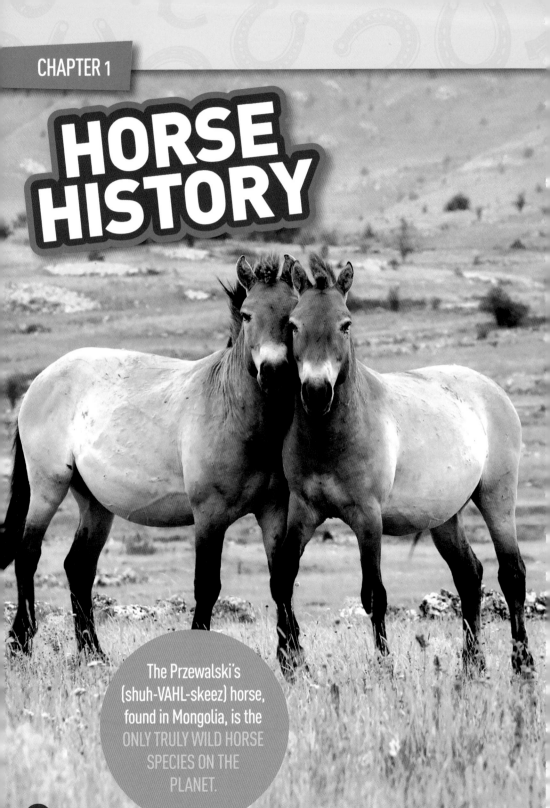

CHAPTER 1

HORSE HISTORY

The Przewalski's (shuh-VAHL-skeez) horse, found in Mongolia, is the ONLY TRULY WILD HORSE SPECIES ON THE PLANET.

Horses and humans have been working together FOR 5,000 YEARS.

The first people to tame wild horses may have been a group of nomads. Nomads are people who travel from place to place, rather than living in one spot. These nomads trained horses to carry people and pull heavy loads through their lands in Asia. This helped them travel farther and faster.

Since then, people around the world have been putting horses to work.

As horses helped humans more and more over the years, humans developed breeds for different jobs. Huge draft horses like Percherons and Belgians plowed fields. Elegant driving horses pulled carriages.

Horses were also used in entertainment and sports. Graceful Lipizzaner horses, one of the oldest breeds in Europe, performed routines of precise, dance-like leaps and kicks. Swift quarter horses and long-legged Thoroughbreds raced for cheering crowds. Many of these breeds still do those jobs today.

ANCIENT GREEKS used horses to race chariots.

Lipizzaner (lip-it-SAHN-ur)

Belgian (BEL-jin)

Percheron (PURCH-ur-on)

There are about 400 DIFFERENT BREEDS of horses in the world.

quarter horse

Thoroughbred (THUR-oh-bred)

HORSES ARE MEASURED IN "HANDS," or units of measurement four inches long.

horse

A pony is a horse SHORTER THAN 14.2 HANDS HIGH at the withers, or shoulders.

pony

10

Ponies have SHORTER LEGS AND OFTEN SMALLER EARS than horses.

Welsh pony

Ponies are small horses. And just as a small adult dog won't grow to be the size of a big dog, a pony will not grow to be a full-size horse. Known for being cute and playful, ponies are also known for being naughty!

Some regions of the world are known for their horses. Robust Hanoverian (han-uh-VEER-ee-un) horses originated 300 years ago in Hanover, Germany. Tough Norwegian Fjords (nore-WEEJ-un FEE-ordz) are from Norway. Lively Arabian horses were first bred by nomads who lived in North Africa and the Arabian Peninsula.

Arabian horses

THE HAFLINGER IS A STURDY AUSTRIAN BREED known for its flaxen (or cream-colored) mane and tail.

Short, stocky Shetland ponies HAULED COAL OUT OF MINES in Scotland in the 1800s.

CHAPTER 2

HORSE SENSE

Horses are HERD ANIMALS. Living in a herd means that horses rely on one another for protection, security, and comfort.

Horses stick together. In a herd that lives in the wild, the lead mare, or female, guides the group to safe places to graze or drink. The lead stallion, or male, often brings up the rear to protect the herd. Horses that live together on a ranch or a farm usually prefer to stay close to one another, too.

Most horses graze in fenced pastures or meadows. Some forage on open land. Human caregivers often feed horses grain or nutritious man–made pellets served in buckets. Most horses also love to munch hay (dried grass).

Horses love to nibble apples, carrots, peppermint candies, sugar cubes, and even GINGERSNAP COOKIES.

If stretched out, a horse's digestive system would be about 100 FEET LONG FROM BEGINNING TO END.

Horses CANNOT THROW UP.

A foal, or baby horse, can stand SHORTLY AFTER BIRTH.

A foal stands soon after it's born so that it can nurse and nuzzle its mother. Wobbly at first, most foals can walk after a few minutes. They stay close to their mother but build confidence quickly. Soon it's time to run and play: Dart! Dash! Buck! Kick!

A YEARLING is a horse that is one year old.

Male foals are called COLTS, while females are called FILLIES.

Icelandic horse

"Gaited" horses—like Missouri Fox Trotters, Tennessee Walking Horses, and Icelandic horses— ARE BRED FOR SUPERSMOOTH GAITS.

No matter what breed or size, all horses and ponies have the same body structure and move in the same way. They have four basic natural gaits, or ways of moving: walk, trot, canter, and gallop. In the trot, two hooves hit the ground at the same time, making two hoofbeats (think *clip-clop*). The canter has a three-hoofbeat rhythm. During the gallop, a horse's fastest pace, all four hooves spring off the ground for an instant during each stride, as if the horse is flying.

trot

canter

gallop

A Thoroughbred's stride at the gallop can be MORE THAN 20 FEET LONG.

Horses Up Close

From nose to tail, check out a horse's amazing body.

Most horses grow a heavier coat in the winter. When the weather warms, horses shed shaggy winter hair and return to their sleek summer coat.

A horse's long tail makes an excellent flyswatter. It also gives signals about how a horse is feeling.

A horse's hind legs are larger and stronger than its front legs. They thrust its body forward and provide power for jumping or climbing hills.

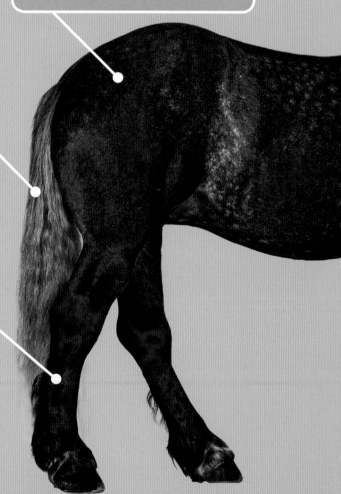

A horse's ears swivel to hear sounds from all directions. When horses walk in a line, they work together to listen for danger. The one in front pricks its ears forward, the one in back turns its ears backward, and those in the middle rotate their ears to the sides.

Horses have the largest eyes of any land mammal. They are eight times the size of human eyes. Because their eyes are on the sides of their head, horses can see in almost every direction.

A horse's strong teeth grind grass and hay. They wear down over time, providing clues about a horse's age.

A horse's hooves protect its legs from the force of running, walking, and standing. Underneath the hoof is a soft, triangular pad called a frog. It acts like a superpowered shock absorber.

Horses' coats vary widely in color—from PALE GOLD to RUSTY RED and shades of BROWN, BLACK, and GRAY.

Horses often have white on their lower legs. Depending on the height of the white, the marks are called socks or stockings. A round white spot between a horse's eyes is called a star. A blaze is a long white mark down its face, and a stripe is a skinny blaze. A snip is a little white mark on its nose. If the white on a horse's face extends past both eyes, the horse is said to have a bald face.

CHESTNUT HORSES are reddish in color.

Most Appaloosa horses are light-colored with spots on their rear end. A "LEOPARD" APPALOOSA HAS SPOTS COVERING ITS ENTIRE BODY.

An eye-catching PINTO is any horse marked with large PATCHES OF WHITE all over its body.

A BAY HORSE HAS A BROWN BODY, black markings on its legs, and a black mane and tail.

Horse Talk

People can learn a lot about horses by listening to how they communicate with each other. They use a variety of sounds to share what they are feeling.

A horse's groan sounds similar to a human's groan and CAN BE A SIGN OF PAIN.

A bugle-like whinny can mean "I'm worried" or "I'm excited." A deep sigh can express relaxation. A loud snort warns other horses of danger.

A foal recognizes its mother BY HER NICKER, or soft whinny.

A horse's SNORT can be heard from 30 FEET AWAY.

A horse's body language says a lot about how it's feeling, too. The flick of a tail may be a warning to stand back. A gentle nudge of its nose might mean "May I please have a carrot?" Even a horse's nostrils help with communication. A gentle puff of air blown in your face is a friendly hello.

Ears flopped to sides: Means the horse is probably asleep or very relaxed

Pawing: Shows that a horse is stressed, bored, or impatient

Hind leg cocked, head down: Means the horse is resting

Head in the air: Signals that the horse sees something in the distance and is deciding how to react

ears flopped to sides

pawing

hind leg cocked, head down

head in the air

29

Super Senses

A horse lifts its upper lip to get a BETTER WHIFF OF AN INTERESTING SMELL.

A horse's sense of smell is THOUSANDS OF TIMES BETTER THAN A HUMAN'S.

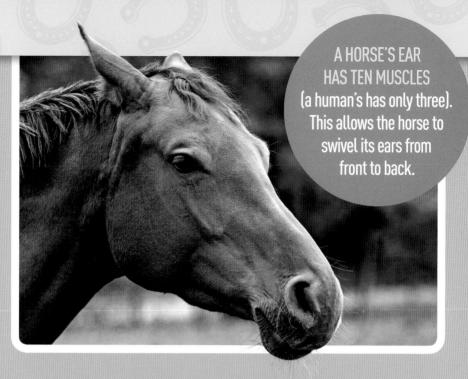

A HORSE'S EAR HAS TEN MUSCLES (a human's has only three). This allows the horse to swivel its ears from front to back.

Keen senses—especially smell and hearing—help warn horses of danger. Even though most horses are big, strong, and fast, they are prey animals. Their senses keep them alert to predators. This is especially important for horses that live in the wild. But even horses that live with humans still have these keen senses and react quickly to danger.

Most of the time, horses are quiet and calm. But they startle easily. So it's important to be careful when you're around these large animals. When you greet a horse, approach from the side and stroke its neck. Speak softly. Don't run, yell, throw things, or wave your arms. Don't walk behind a horse where it can't see you and might kick out if startled.

Sometimes RACEHORSES ARE FITTED WITH EARPLUGS to quiet scary noises at the course, such as loud vehicles or cheering fans.

➡ Some horse earplugs look like fuzzy pom-poms.

Most horses weigh between 500 AND 2,200 POUNDS.

Big Jake, a 17-year-old Belgian draft horse from Wisconsin, U.S.A., is the tallest horse in the world. HE'S ALMOST SEVEN FEET TALL AT THE SHOULDER.

CHAPTER 3

SADDLE UP!

Since the first time humans saw horses, they've admired the animals for their beauty, strength, and power. Horses are important to people not just for the work they can do, but for the companionship they offer. Why do people love horses so much? And why are horses so loyal to their owners? When a horse and a person trust each other, they create a special bond.

People in the United States spend about $39 BILLION ON HORSES AND THEIR CARE EACH YEAR.

There are approximately 9.2 MILLION HORSES IN THE UNITED STATES, and about one million of them live in Texas.

Horse Care

CURRY COMBS, GROOMING MITTS, AND HOOF PICKS are used to clean horses before and after riding.

THE WORD "TACK" REFERS TO THE EQUIPMENT USED to ride or drive a horse, such as a halter, bridle, and saddle.

It's a lot of work to keep horses healthy, happy, and fit. Every day, horses must be fed and their stalls must be cleaned. Their tack must be kept in good condition.

Vets give horses regular checkups. They also help if a horse is sick or injured. A farrier (FARE-ee-ur) trims a horse's growing hooves and replaces its shoes about once every six weeks. Dentists help keep horses' teeth healthy.

← Using a hoof pick to clean rocks and dirt from a horse's hooves after riding keeps the horse's feet healthy.

Horses are smart animals and learn new things easily. A foal first learns to wear a halter and walk with its trainer on a lead rope. A young horse also learns manners, like how to stand quietly for a bath or pick up its hooves for cleaning.

Later, a trainer can teach it to carry a saddle and rider. With patience and gentle training, a horse can learn to do many things, like perform tricks, herd cattle, or complete a course of jumps.

Horses can learn to RESPOND TO VOICE COMMANDS, such as "walk" to move forward, "whoa" to stop, and "UP" TO REAR UP.

Cool Horse Jobs

OFFICER BARNEY, A RETIRED POLICE HORSE, works at Days End Farm Horse Rescue, helping teach the public about homeless horses.

New York City's police horses live in stables on the ground floor of a LUXURY APARTMENT BUILDING NEAR TIMES SQUARE.

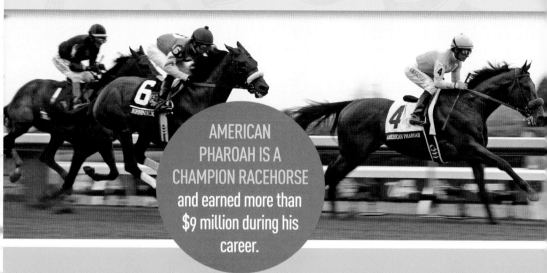

AMERICAN PHAROAH IS A CHAMPION RACEHORSE and earned more than $9 million during his career.

Lots of horses have cool jobs, like Gisele the therapy horse. She's a miniature horse, so she's a handy size for visiting senior citizens and children with special needs. She makes people smile all day long! In New Zealand, a horse named George has a glamorous job as a unicorn. George wears a fake horn and has appeared in movies, television shows, and commercials.

George

George played the unicorn in *The Chronicles of Narnia: The Lion, the Witch and the Wardrobe.*

Even in her 90s, Britain's QUEEN ELIZABETH often starts her day riding her ROYAL FELL PONY, Carltonlima Emma.

Sometimes a horse's job is just to be a friend. It's good for humans, too. Riding and working with horses can be fun, relaxing, and good exercise. In return, most horses only ask for kindness and care, and maybe a carrot or two.

HORSES CAN TELL HOW A PERSON IS FEELING by reading body language and facial expressions.

a Tibetan woman with her horse

1

Cloth covers can be put over a horse's ears to keep flies out.

2

The word "mustang" comes from the Spanish word *mustengo*, which means "stray horse."

3

Back when horses pulled delivery wagons, the horses would often memorize their routes and remember their favorite customers.

4

A horse usually breathes only through its nose and takes about 10 to 12 breaths per minute.

5

Many horses that compete around the world travel in airplanes, snacking on hay and drinking water sweetened with apple juice.

6

In Indiana, U.S.A., a horse named Justin paints on canvas, holding a paintbrush in his mouth.

7

In 1904, a horse named Beautiful Jim Key performed his skills in reading, spelling, and math at the St. Louis World's Fair.

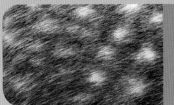

8

Dapples—faint spots on a horse's coat—are a sign of good health.

9

The most expensive saddle ever sold was bought for more than $650,000.

10

Horses with white skin can get sunburned, especially on their nose, where they have little hair.

25 MORE FACTS ABOUT HORSES

11

Some kids compete in horseless horse shows, galloping through a course of jumps on their own two feet.

12

Arabian horses are known to carry their tails high, like flags.

13

Four bronze horseshoes were found in a tomb in Italy and dated to around 400 B.C.

14

Some show horses are dressed up with fake tails for good looks.

15

Some horses have "feathers," long hair that grows at the bottoms of their legs and sometimes over their hooves.

16

When they drink, horses don't lap up water like cats or dogs. They suction water through their lips like a pump.

17

American Pharoah's name contains a spelling error. Can you find it?

18

In cold weather, the heat created from digesting hay helps keep a horse warm from the inside out.

19

A hot walker is a person (or a machine) who walks a racehorse to cool it down after a workout.

20

The forelock is the part of a horse's mane that grows forward from in between its ears.

21

Trigger, the famous golden stallion ridden by movie star cowboy Roy Rogers, appeared in 90 movies and more than 100 television shows.

22

The skeleton of a famous racehorse named Sysonby is on display at the American Museum of Natural History in New York City.

23

Horses usually live to be about 25 to 30 years old.

24

A miniature horse named Tater Tot is a therapy animal with his own special minivan to take him on visits.

25

In Germany and Switzerland, it's against the law to trim a horse's whiskers.

HORSE FACTS ROUNDUP

WHOA!
You've raced through all the equine essentials.
DID YOU CATCH ALL 100 FACTS?

1. Horses can sleep standing up, locking their legs to keep from falling. 2. The oldest known horse lived to be 62 years old. 3. Like most mammals, horses have a belly button. 4. A horse's teeth take up more space in its head than its brain does. 5. Closely related to rhinos and tapirs, horses belong to a group of mammals that have an odd number of toes. 6. Horses belong to the equine family, which also includes zebras, donkeys, and mules. 7. A horse's brain weighs about the same as a human child's—about a pound and a half. 8. The term "equine" refers to a horse or describes things having to do with horses. It comes from the ancient Greek word *equus*, which means "quickness." 9. In the late 1800s, European carriage horses wore straw hats to help shade them in the summer.

10. Tough Welsh ponies roamed the hills and valleys of Wales, Great Britain, as far back as 1600 B.C. 11. Horses with blue eyes are rare, but they can occur in many breeds. 12. Horses tend to move faster when they are headed home. 13. As many as eight million horses served during World War II. 14. An adult horse produces about 10 gallons of saliva per day. 15. At a world-famous riding school in Vienna, Austria, a stallion is referred to as a "professor" once he's finished his training. 16. Blueskin and Nelson were two of General George Washington's war horses during the American Revolution. 17. Many homeless horses around the world are waiting to be adopted. 18. Some horses have wardrobes that include rainproof sheets and fitted blankets. 19. Until the invention of the steam engine in 1698, horses provided the fastest and most reliable transportation on land. 20. A horse's hooves grow about a quarter inch per month. 21. The famous racehorse Exterminator had a series of companion ponies, all named Peanuts. 22. Some birds like to make nests out of discarded horse hair. 23. Horses carried gear across the Rocky Mountains for Meriwether Lewis and William Clark. 24. In the timed sport of barrel racing, horse and rider race a cloverleaf pattern around a set of three barrels. 25. Male horses have more teeth than females do, including four extra "fighting teeth." 26. The Przewalski's horse is the only truly wild horse species on the planet. 27. Some cave art depicting horses dates back to around 36,000 B.C. 28. Horses and humans have been working together for 5,000 years. 29. Ancient Greeks used horses to race chariots. 30. There are about 400 different breeds of horses in the world. 31. Horses are measured in "hands," or units of measurement four inches long. 32. A pony is a horse shorter than 14.2 hands high at the withers. 33. Ponies have shorter legs and often smaller ears than horses. 34. Horses can be found just about anywhere in the world. 35. The Haflinger is a sturdy Austrian breed known for its flaxen mane and tail. 36. Short, stocky Shetland ponies hauled coal out of mines in Scotland in the 1800s. 37. Horses are herd animals. This means they rely on one another for protection, security, and comfort. 38. A pair of horses will often stand nose to tail, each swatting flies from the other's face. 39. Half of the wild horses in the United States live in the deserts and mountains of Nevada. 40. Horses' main food is grass, which means they are herbivores. 41. Horses love to nibble apples, sugar cubes, and

even gingersnap cookies. **42.** If stretched out, a horse's digestive system would be about 100 feet long from beginning to end. **43.** Horses cannot throw up. **44.** When a foal is born, its legs are almost as long as its adult legs will be. **45.** A foal can stand shortly after birth. **46.** A yearling is a horse that is one year old. **47.** Male foals are called colts, while females are called fillies. **48.** "Gaited" horses are bred for supersmooth gaits. **49.** A Thoroughbred's stride at the gallop can be more than 20 feet long. **50.** Horses' coats vary widely in color—from pale gold to black. **51.** Chestnut horses are reddish in color. **52.** Most Appaloosa horses are light-colored with spots on their rear end. A "leopard" Appaloosa has spots covering its entire body. **53.** A pinto is any horse marked with large patches of white all over its body. **54.** A bay horse has a brown body, black markings on its legs, and a black mane and tail. **55.** A horse's groan sounds similar to a human's groan and can be a sign of pain. **56.** A foal recognizes its mother by her nicker. **57.** A horse's snort can be heard from 30 feet away. **58.** A horse lifts its upper lip to get a better whiff of an interesting smell. **59.** A horse's sense of smell is thousands of times better than a human's. **60.** A horse's ear has ten muscles (a human's has only three). **61.** If a horse senses danger, its first instinct is to flee. **62.** Sometimes racehorses are fitted with earplugs to quiet scary noises at the course. **63.** Most horses weigh between 500 and 2,200 pounds. **64.** Big Jake, a 17-year-old Belgian draft horse, is the tallest horse in the world. He's almost seven feet tall at the shoulder. **65.** People in the United States spend about $39 billion on horses and their care each year. **66.** There are approximately 9.2 million horses in the United States, and about one million of them live in Texas. **67.** Curry combs, grooming mitts, and hoof picks are used to clean horses before and after riding. **68.** The word "tack" refers to the equipment used to ride or drive a horse. **69.** A "green" horse isn't really green, it's inexperienced. **70.** Horses can learn to respond to voice commands, such as "up" to rear up. **71.** Officer Barney, a retired police horse, helps teach the public about homeless horses. **72.** New York City's police horses live in stables on the ground floor of a luxury apartment building near Times Square. **73.** American Pharoah is a champion racehorse and earned more than $9 million during his career. **74.** Britain's Queen Elizabeth often starts her day riding her Royal Fell pony. **75.** Horses can tell how a person is feeling by reading body language and facial expressions. **76.** Cloth covers can be put over a horse's ears to keep flies out. **77.** The word "mustang" comes from the Spanish word *mustengo*, which means "stray horse." **78.** Horses that pulled delivery wagons would often memorize their routes and remember their favorite customers. **79.** A horse usually breathes only through its nose and takes about 10 to 12 breaths per minute. **80.** Many horses that compete around the world travel in airplanes, snacking on hay and drinking water sweetened with apple juice. **81.** In Indiana, U.S.A., a horse named Justin paints on canvas, holding a paintbrush in his mouth. **82.** In 1904, a horse named Beautiful Jim Key performed his skills in reading, spelling, and math at the St. Louis World's Fair. **83.** Dapples—faint spots on a horse's coat—are a sign of good health. **84.** The most expensive saddle ever sold was bought for more than $650,000. **85.** Horses with white skin can get sunburned. **86.** Some kids compete in horseless horse shows, galloping through a course of jumps on their own two feet. **87.** Arabian horses are known to carry their tails high, like flags. **88.** Four bronze horseshoes were found in a tomb in Italy and dated to around 400 B.C. **89.** Some show horses are dressed up with fake tails for good looks. **90.** Some horses have "feathers," long hair that grows at the bottoms of their legs and sometimes over their hooves. **91.** When they drink, horses suction water through their lips like a pump. **92.** American Pharoah's name contains a spelling error. Can you find it? **93.** In cold weather, the heat created from digesting hay helps keep a horse warm from the inside out. **94.** A hot walker is a person (or a machine) who walks a racehorse to cool it down after a workout. **95.** The forelock is the part of a horse's mane that grows forward from in between its ears. **96.** Trigger, the famous golden stallion ridden by Roy Rogers, appeared in 90 movies and more than 100 television shows. **97.** The skeleton of a famous racehorse named Sysonby is on display at the American Museum of Natural History. **98.** Horses usually live to be about 25 to 30 years old. **99.** A miniature horse named Tater Tot is a therapy animal with his own special minivan to take him on visits. **100.** In Germany and Switzerland, it's against the law to trim a horse's whiskers.

INDEX

Boldface indicates illustrations.

A
Appaloosa horses 25, **25**
Arabian horses 12, **12–13,** 45

B
Barrel racing 5
Belgian horses 8, **9,** 33, **33**
Body language 28–29, 43

C
Cave art 7, **7**
Colts 19

D
Dapples 44, **44**
Draft horses 8, **9,** 33, **33**

E
Earplugs 33, **33**
Elizabeth II, Queen (United Kingdom) 42, **42**

F
Fillies 19
Flies 15, 44, **44**
Foals 18–19, **18–19,** 27, **27,** 38
Forelocks 45, **45**

G
Gaits 20, **21**
Grass 16, 23
Greeks, ancient 8, **8**

H
Haflinger horses 13, **13**
Hay 16, **16,** 23, 44, 45, **45**
Herd animals 14, 15
Homeless animals 5, 40
Hooves 5, 20, 23, **23,** 37, **37,** 38
Horses
  brain 4, **4**
  care of 36–37, **37, 38,** 42
  coats 22, 24
  communication 26–28
  digestive system 17, 45
  ears 11, 23, **23,** 29, **29,** 31, **31,** 44
  eyes 5, **5,** 23, **23**
  food 16–17, **16–17**
  noses 28, **28,** 44
  sleep 4, 29
  tails 15, **15,** 22, **22,** 28, 45, **45**

  teeth 4, 5, **5,** 23, 37
  weight 33
Horseshoes 37, **37, 44,** 45

I
Icelandic horses 20, **20**

J
Jobs for horses 8, **40–41,** 40–42

L
Lipizzaner horses 8, **9**

M
Miniature horses 41, 45

N
Nomads 7, 12

P
Percherons 8, **9**
Police horses 40, **40**
Ponies 5, **10,** 11, **11, 13,** 20, **42**
Przewalski's horses 6, **6**

Q
Quarter horses 8, **9**

R
Racehorses 5, 33, **33, 41,** 45

S
Saddles **36,** 38, 44
Shetland ponies 13, **13**
Smell, sense of 30, 31

T
Therapy animals 41, 45
Thoroughbreds 8, **9,** 21
Training 5, 7, 38, 39

V
Vienna, Austria: riding school **5**

W
Washington, George 5
Welsh ponies 5, **11**
World War II 5

Y
Yearlings 19

Z
Zebras 4, **4**